# Timeless Seeds of Advice to a Friend

Imam Ibn Qayyim al-Jawziyya

# About This Book

In this short yet substantial book, Imam Ibn al-Qayyim al-Jawziyyah pens a beautiful message of heartfelt advice to his friend Al-Din. He invokes Allah's Kindness, Guidance and Blessing upon him.

The author explains the need in seeking Allah's Guidance in life, in all of our affairs and the means to persist upon the Good and Straight Path. The knowledge-based content of this book shows the Imam's attention to detail. He explains everything in an easy to understand manner.

The book is modelled as sincere advice to his friend that will of course, be of wider benefit to all who read it, if God is willing. The Imam says that if you come to know what he have explained (in this message), then you will know that the ultimate pleasure, perfect delight and rejoice, grace and good life are found only in the Straight Path and worshipping Allah alone. And only then you will feel comfort and the longing for the afterlife and to meeting Him, the Merciful, the Most Merciful.

**I have never regretted anything as much as my regret over a day on which the sun had set and my life span had decreased while my good deeds have not increased a bit**

**Ibn Masud (RadiyAllahlu anhu)**

"Sins have many side-effects. One of them is that they steal knowledge from you."

"There is no captive in a worse state than the one who is captivated by his worst enemy (Shaytan) and there is no prison which is tighter than the prison of hawa (desire) and there is no bond/fetter more strong than the bond of desire. How, then, will a heart which is captivated, imprisoned and fettered travel unto Allah and the Home of the Hereafter?"

"As long as you are performing prayer, you are knocking at the door of Allah, and whoever is knocking at the door of Allah, Allah will open it for him."

"When a person spends his entire day with no concern but Allah alone, Allah will take care of all his needs and take care of all that is worrying him; He will empty his heart so that it will be filled only with love for Him."

"If a man's patience is stronger than his whims and desires, then he is like an angel, but if his whims and desires are stronger than his patience, then he is like a devil. If his desire for food, drink and sex is stronger than his patience, then he is no better than an animal."

-- Ibn Al-Qayyim

"The heart, in its journey to Allah, Majestic is He, is like that of a bird; Love is its head, and fear and hope are its two wings. When the head and two wings are sound, the bird flies gracefully; if the head is severed, the bird dies; if the bird loses one of its wings, it then becomes a target for every hunter or predator."

"Truly in the heart there is a void that can not be removed except with the company of Allah. And in it there is a sadness that can not be removed except with the happiness of knowing Allah and being true to Him. And in it there is an emptiness that can not be filled except with love for Him and by turning to Him and always remembering Him. And if a person were given all of the world and what is in it, it would not fill this emptiness."

"Satan rejoiced when Adam (peace be upon him) came out of Paradise, but he did not know that when a diver sinks into the sea, he collects pearls and then rises again."

"This wordly life is like a shadow. If you try to catch it, you will never be able to do so. If you turn your back towards it, it has no choice but to follow you."

"Losing time is harder than death, as losing time keeps you away from Allah and the Hereafter, while death keeps you away from the worldly life and people."

-- Ibn AL-Qayyim

# Content

# Imam Ibn Qayyim al-Jawziyya

# May Allah have mercy upon him

## His Name:

HE IS THE IMĀM, THE ḤĀFIẒ, the exegete, the legal jurist, Shaykh al-Islām: Abū 'Abdullāh Shamsu-d-Dīn Muḥammad Ibn Abū Bakr - better known as Ibn Qayyim al-Jawziyyah.

## His Birth and Education:

He was born into a noble and knowledgeable family on 7th Safar 691H in the village of Zar', near Damascus, Syria.

From an early age he set about acquiring knowledge of the Islāmic sciences from the scholars of his time. Describing his desire for knowledge, al-Ḥāfiẓ Ibn Rajab, *Dhayl Ṭabaqāt-l-Ḥanābilah* [4/449] said, 'He had an intense love for knowledge, for books, publications and writings.'

Ibn Kathīr, *al-Bidāyah wa-n-Nihāyah* [14/235] said, 'He acquired from such books what others could not acquire, and he developed a deep understanding of the books of the Salaf and of the Khalaf.'

## His Teachers and Shaykhs:

They include Shihāb an-Nāblusī, Qāḍī Taqī ad-Dīn ibn Sulaymān, from whom he studied ḥadīth; Qāḍī Badr ad-Dīn ibn Jamā'ah; Ṣafī ad-Dīn al-Hindī; Ismā'īl ibn Muḥammad al-Ḥarrānī, from whom he studied fiqh and usūl; and also his father, from whom he learnt the laws of inheritance.

However, the most notable of his teachers was Shaykh al-Islām Ibn Taymiyyah, whom he accompanied and studied under for sixteen years. Al-Ḥāfiẓ Ibn Kathīr (14/234) said, 'He attained great proficiency in many branches of knowledge; particularly knowledge of tafsīr, ḥadīth, and usūl. When Shaykh Taqī ad-Dīn ibn Taymiyyah returned from Egypt in the year 712H, he stayed with the Shaykh until he died; learning a great deal of knowledge from him, along with the knowledge that he had already occupied himself in attaining. So he became a unique scholar in many branches of knowledge.'

## His Manners and Worship:

Many of his students and contemporaries have born witness to his excellent character and his manners of worship. Ibn Rajab (4/450) said,

> He - may Allāh have mercy on him - was constant in worship and performing the night prayer, reaching the limits in lengthening his prayer and devotion. He

> was constantly in a state of *dhikr* and had an intense love for Allāh. He also had a deep love for turning to Allāh in repentance, humbling himself to Him with a deep sense of humility and helplessness. He would throw himself at the doors of Divine obedience and servitude. Indeed, I have not seen the likes of him with regards to such matters.

Ibn Kathīr (14/234) said,

> He was constant in humbly entreating and calling upon his Lord. He recited well and had fine manners. He had a great deal of love and did not harbour any envy or malice towards anyone, nor did he seek to harm or find fault with them. I was one of those who most often kept company with him and was one of the most beloved of people to him. I do not know of anyone in the world in this time, who is a greater worshipper than him. His prayer used to be very lengthy, with prolonged bowing and prostrations. His colleagues would criticise him for this, yet he never retorted back, nor did he abandon this practice. May Allāh bestow His mercy upon him.

## His Students and Works:

Amongst his most prominent students were: Ibn Kathīr (d.774H), adh-Dhahabī (d.748H), Ibn Rajab (d.751H) and Ibn 'Abdu-l-Hādī (d.744H), as well as two of his sons, Ibrāhīm and Sharafu-d-Dīn 'Abdullāh.

Ibnu-l-Qayyim authored over sixty works. His books and writings are characterised by their touching address to the heart and soul, as well as their accuracy, precision, strength of argument and depth of research.

In the field of fiqh and usūl, his writings include: *I'lāmu-l-Muwaqqiḥīn; Turuqu-l-Ḥukmiyyah; Ighāthatu-l-Lahfān; Tuḥfatu-l-Mawlūd; Aḥkām Ahlu-l-Dhimmah*; and *al-Furūsiyyah.*

In the field of ḥadīth and sīrah they include: *Tahdhīb Sunan Abī Dāwūd; al-Manāru-l-Munīf; Fawā'id al-Ḥadīthiyyah; Jalā'u-l-Afhām; and Zādu-l-Ma'ād.*

In the field of beliefs: *Ijtimā' al-Juyūsh al-Islāmiyyah; as-Ṣawā'iqu-l-Mursalah; Shifā'u-l-'Alīl; Ḥādiyu-l-Arwāḥ; al-Kāfiyatu-sh-Shāfiyah*; and *Kitāb ar-Rūḥ.*

In the field of akhlāq (morals) and tazkiyah (purification): *Madāriju-s-Sālikīn; ad-Dā' wa-d-Dawā'; al-Wābilu-s-Ṣayyib; al-Fawā'id; Risālatu-t-Tabūkiyyah; Miftāḥ Dār as-Sa'ādah*; and *'Uddatu-s-Ṣābirīn.*

In the sciences of the Qur'ān: *at-Tibyān fi Aqsāmi-l-Qur'ān*; and *Amthāl al-Qur'ān.*

In language and miscellaneous issues: *Badā'i al-Fawā'id.*

Two books have also been written collating the exegetical comments of ibn al-Qayyim from his various works: *Tafsīr al-Qayyim* and *Tafsīr al-Munīr.*

A few of his works have also been translated into the English language: Paragons of the Qur'an; Trails and Tribulations; Characteristics of the Hypocrites and Inner Dimentions of the Prayer.

## Statements of the Scholars about him:

Ibn Rajab (4/44) said,

> He had deep knowledge concerning tafsīr and the fundamentals of the religion, reaching the highest degree concerning them both. Similar was the case in the field of ḥadīth, with regards to understanding its meanings, subtleties and deducing rulings from them. Likewise was the case in the field of fiqh and its usūl, as well as the Arabic language. He did a great service to these sciences. He was also knowledgeable about rhetoric, grammar, and *sulūk* as well as the subtleties and details that occur in the speech of the people of *tasawwuf*.

Al-Ḥāfiẓ Ibn Ḥajar, *ad-Duraru-l-Kāminah* (4/21),

> He possessed a courageous spirit as well as vast and comprehensive knowledge. He had deep knowledge concerning the differences of opinions of the Scholars and about the ways of the Salaf.

Ibn Ḥajar also said in his commendation to ar-Raddu-l-Wāfir,

> And if there were no virtues of Shaykh Taqī ad-Dīn [Ibn Taymiyyah], except for his famous student, Shaykh Shamsu-d-Dīn ibn Qayyim al-Jawziyyah - the author of many works, which both his opponents and supporters benefited from - this would be a sufficient indication of his [Ibn Taymiyyah's] great position.

al-Ḥāfiẓ Ibn Nāṣir ad-Dimishqī, *ar-Raddu-l-Wāfir* [p. 69] said,

> He possessed knowledge of the sciences, especially

tafsīr and usūl.

He also said:

> Abū Bakr Muḥammad Ibn al-Muhib said, as found in his letter, "I said in front of our Shaykh, al-Mizzī, 'Is Ibnu-l-Qayyim at the same level as Ibn Khuzaymah?' He replied, 'He is in this time, what Ibn Khuzaymah was in his time.'"

As-Suyūṭī, *Bughyatu-l-Wiʿāt* [1/62] said,

> His books had no equal and he strove and became one of the great Imāms in [the field of] tafsīr, ḥadīth, the Book, the Sunnah, furūʿ, and the Arabic language.

ʿAlī al-Qārī, *al-Mirqāt* [8/251],

> It will be clear to whoever aspires to read the explanation of *Manāzilu-s-Sāʾirīn* [i.e. *Madārij as-Sālikīn*], that they [Ibn Taymiyyah and Ibnu-l-Qayyim] are from the great ones of *Ahlu-s-Sunnah wa-l-Jamāʿah*, and from the *awliyāʾ* of this Ummah.

Qāḍī Burhān ad-Dīn az-Zurʿā said as quoted from him in *Dhayl Ṭabaqāt al-Ḥanābilah*,

> There is none under the heavens who has greater knowledge than he.

# His Death:

Imām Ibnu-l-Qayyim passed away at the age of sixty, on the 13th night of Rajab, 751H, may Allāh shower His Mercy upon him.

# Introduction

## With the Name of Allah, the All-Merciful, the Most Merciful

IMĀM MUḤAMMAD IBN ABĪ BAKR Ibn Qayyim al-Jawziyyah, may Allāh bestow His Mercy upon him, said:

I ask Allāh, in Whom I have hope to answer our prayers, to embrace the brother 'Alā' Al-Dīn with His Kindness in this life and the Afterlife; to make him a source of benefit [to others]; and to make him blessed wherever may he be - for indeed, the *barakah* of a man lies in his teaching of the good wherever he may land and in his advices to every person he meets. In the Qur'ān, the *ayah* wherein Allāh, Most High, informs us of what Prophet 'Īsā (*'alayhis-salām*) said about himself, reads as follows:

وَجَعَلَنِي مُبَارَكًا أَيْنَ مَا كُنتُ

"And He has made me blessed wherever I am"

[*Maryam* (19): 31]

This is to mean, He made me [i.e. 'Īsā] a teacher of goodness, a caller to Allāh, and an advocate who reminds people of Allāh and spurs them to obey Him. Truly, all those qualities are from the *barakah* of a man! If a person lacks the said qualities, not only is he devoid of *barakah*, but also there will be no such *barakah* when meeting him or being with him.

## [i. The Value of Time]

Further, the absence of *barakah* will extend to throw its shades on whoever meets him or be in his company because such a person wastes his time talking about [trivial] current affairs and past events that cause the heart [of his company] to be ruined and clouded for it is the waste of time and the corruption of the heart (*fasād al-qalb*) that are the prime causes of all types of harm befalling people. Not only does that make a person lose his share of reward, but it will also lower his rank (*darajah*) and status (*manzila*) in the sight of Allāh.

It is for this reason, some scholars advised, "Beware of mixing with those whose company will waste your time and corrupt your heart, lest otherwise all your affairs be ruined and you become among those whom Allāh said about in the Qur'ān,

وَلَا تُطِعْ مَنْ أَغْفَلْنَا قَلْبَهُۥ عَن ذِكْرِنَا وَٱتَّبَعَ هَوَىٰهُ وَكَانَ أَمْرُهُۥ فُرُطًا ﴿٢٨﴾

> "And do not obey one whose heart We have made heedless of Our remembrance and who follows his desire and whose affair is ever [in] neglect."
>
> [*al-Kahf* (18): 28]"

If you contemplate the state and conditions of this type of people, you will find the heart of all of them, except maybe a few, is in a state of heedlessness (*ghafla*) and being led by their whims and desires (*al-hawā*), until their affair becomes ever negligent (فُرُطًا); hence they observe not what benefits their hearts and increases their righteousness; and they engage in matters that not only bring them no benefit, but may also cause them harm sooner or later.[1]

Allāh, Exalted be He, ordered His Messenger (ﷺ) not to obey this group. Thus, the obedience of the Prophet (ﷺ) necessitated not to obey this group of people because they call for the following of desires and for neglecting the remembrance of Allāh.

## [ii. Heedlessness (*al-ghafla*) and Desire (*al-hawā*)]

If heedlessness (*al-ghafla*) of Allāh and the Hereafter is coupled with following ones' own whims and desires (*ittibā' al-hawā*), then only evil emanates from such a relation - and it is often that both exist hand in hand and never are apart from each other.

If a person ponders on the corrupt state of the world, in general and in particular, one will understand that heedlessness stands as a barrier between the servant [of Allāh] and understanding and knowing Allāh. Following of whims and desires keep one away from searching for the truth and following it. In the case of the former, such a person becomes from those who are astray, and in the case of the latter, he becomes among those upon whom Allāh evoked His Anger.

## [iii.The Favoured Ones]

In contrast, those to whom Allāh conferred His Favour upon are those that He has guided to acquire knowledge about Him, then submit to Him, and prefer Him over everything else. Truly, those are the ones who embarked the path of safety while the rest are walking on the road of doom. It is for this reason, Allāh ordered us to recite every day and every night for a number of times [during the *ṣalāh*],

اهْدِنَا الصِّرَاطَ الْمُسْتَقِيمَ ﴿٦﴾ صِرَاطَ الَّذِينَ أَنْعَمْتَ
عَلَيْهِمْ غَيْرِ الْمَغْضُوبِ عَلَيْهِمْ وَلَا الضَّالِّينَ ﴿٧﴾

> "Guide us to the straight path - The path of those upon whom You have bestowed favor, not of those who have evoked [Your] anger or of those who are astray."
> [*al-Fātiḥah* (1): 6-7]

To be among those whom are guided by Allāh to the right path - the servant of Allāh is in great need to know all that which will benefit him in this life and the Hereafter; to be inclined to favour what will benefit him over anything else, and to avoid all that which harms him [in this life and the Hereafter]. If however, one overlooks knowledge, they will then be embarking upon a path of those who are astray, and if one deviates, does not comply nor submits to Allāh, one will then be treading on the path of those whom Allāh is angry with. By this elucidation, it becomes clear [to us] the high-status and significance of this supplication and prayer, and the great need of people to have it fulfilled in their lives as the happiness of a person in this life and the Hereafter depends on it.

The servants need [of Allāh] for guidance is always persisting in all affairs; with every breath one takes, every moment one lives, and [the need for having this supplication be answered] manifests in every affair, be that in all that one receives or all that one leaves - for one cannot but to be:

i. A person whose ignorance made him to believe in matters or to perform actions that contravene the guidance [of Islām]; hence he needs to seek Allāh's guidance about these matters.

ii. A person who is aware of the guidance [of Islām about some matters] but, nevertheless, he intentionally contravenes it; hence, he needs to repent from it [i.e. the sin].

iii. A person who lacks guidance [on particular matters] at both levels, knowledge and action; therefore he fails to acquire the knowledge and to act upon its purpose [accordingly].

iv. A person whose guidance on some matters is incomplete i.e. he is guided only to some aspects of a matter; hence he needs to perfect and complete his guidance.

v. A person whose guidance does not extend to cover the details of the matters he is guided to; hence he needs guidance on these details.

vi. A person who is guided to find the [directions to the] right path but that requires him to have guidance again after he embarks upon it, because to be guided to [find] the right path is one thing and to be guided after proceeding in the path is another thing. For example, a person may know the directions to a particular town but he cannot travel the journey because to do that, he needs to have guidance on how to make the journey, such as knowing the best time for travelling, knowing the quantity of water needed for the trip and knowing where to rest during the journey and etc. If the latter guidance is not acquired, the traveler may suffer or die during the trip.

vii. A person who needs to have future guidance on some matters just as he had guidance on such matters in the past.

viii. A person who holds no view on some matters so he neither believes them to be false nor true; hence he needs to be guided to the right belief about them.

ix. A person who believes he is guided in some matters while, in fact, he is astray without realising it; hence he needs to change his position, which cannot be except by the guidance of Allāh.

x. A person who is guided to some matters and yet also needs guiding, advising and directing others to what he was guided to as this will maintain his guidance; otherwise he may be deprived from it. This is because as the known proverb states, *"like the fault, like the punishment"* i.e. as a person guides and teaches others, Allāh will guide him and teach him to become a rightly guided person who guides others too. This is a rank that was narrated in the supplication of the Prophet (ﷺ), who said:

> "O Allāh, adorn us with the beauty of *īmān* (faith), make us rightly guided who guide others; do not let us astray or lead others astray, let us be peaceful with your supporters and belligerent with your enemies, make us love those who love You for they love You; and let us show enmity against those who disobey your Command."[2]

[2] Ṣaḥīḥ Ibn Khuzaymah, #1119
It was declared ḍaʿīf by Albānī, *Ḍaʿīf al-Jāmiʿ* #1194

Allāh, Exalted be He, has praised His believing servants who beseech Him to be people who are rightly guided, and who stand out as role models for others to follow in their guidance; He said in the *ayah*,

وَالَّذِينَ يَقُولُونَ رَبَّنَا
هَبْ لَنَا مِنْ أَزْوَاجِنَا وَذُرِّيَّاتِنَا قُرَّةَ أَعْيُنٍ وَاجْعَلْنَا
لِلْمُتَّقِينَ إِمَامًا ﴿٧٤﴾

> "And those who say, 'Our Lord, grant us from among our wives and offspring comfort to our eyes and make us an example for the righteous.'"
>
> [*al-Furqān* (25) :74]

Ibn 'Abbās (*raḍiyAllāhu 'anhuma*) said commenting, "It means, [O Allāh] make people guided to the good through us",

Abū Ṣālih commented, "It means, let people be guided through our guidance."

Makhūl said, "[It means] let us be examples in righteousness so that the righteous follow our example."

Mujāhid commented, "[It means, O Allāh] make us followers of the righteous ones and [let us] follow their example in righteousness."

The explanation of Mujāhid was found problematic by *those who did not comprehend the knowledge of the righteous predecessors or realise the depth of knowledge they had.* For this reason, they objected by arguing that, "According to his explanation, the meaning of the *ayah* will be reversed to mean, [O Allāh] make the righteous be the example we follow."

I take refuge in Allāh from such a statement because it is impossible to find any *ayah* with a reversed meaning in the Qur'ān, because the statement of Mujāhid, may Allāh engulf him with His Mercy, indicates his perfect comprehension since it is obvious that a person cannot be an example that the righteous follow his leads unless he himself follows the example of the righteous ones.

This is the aspect that Mujāhid intended to highlight, which explains how a person can attain this high rank - that is by following the example of the righteous people who preceded him so as Allāh makes the righteous ones succeeding him in time to follow his example. Truly, this is from the best understanding of Qur'ān and [as explained] it is irrelevant to the issue of *"reversed meaning."*

That being the case, whoever follows the example of the predecessors who adhered to the Sunnah, his example will be followed by those who succeed him in time and also by those who live in the same era of his.

The word (إِمَامًا) *"Imām"* - translated to *"an example for"* is used in its singular form; and as can be noted, Allāh, Most High, did not use the plural form of the work as the *ayah* did not read to say, *"Make us examples for the righteous."*

This has been explained by many scholars, some of whom explained that the word *"Imām"* is the plural of the word *"Aām"*, but this interpretation is farfetched and uncommon to be found in the famous usage of Arabic language; hence such understanding cannot be used to interpret or explain the words of Allāh. Other scholars said, the word *"Imām"* is not an *ism* (i.e. a gerund) but rather a *masdar* (i.e. a noun that is derived from a verb and usually preserves the verb's syntactic features); hence it implies the meaning, "*make us to have an Imām*", and this interpretation is an ever weaker opinion than the aforesaid one.

Al-Farrā said, "the reason why the word *"Imām"* was used in a singular format; and not plural, is because it falls under the category of the singular that is intended to refer to a plural just like the word *'messenger'* used in the *ayah*, *"We are the Messenger of the Lord of worlds"* wherein the word used is singular though it refers to two persons. This interpretation is the best of all but still requires further elucidation - that is: All the righteous people walk in the same path, worship the same illah (God), adhere to the same Book, believe in the same Prophet, and they are all the servants of One Lord i.e. their religion is the same, their Prophet is the same, their divine Book is the same and the illah they worship is the same; hence it is as if all of this makes out the Imām that they follow. This is the absolute opposite of the case of Imāms whose views, paths, beliefs, creed and methodology are different. Thus in reality, following the example of the righteous means following what they are upon.

# Chapter One

# Patience (al-sabr) and Certainty (al-yaqin)

Allāh, Most High, informed us that the state of being an Imām in religion [i.e. a righteous person who people take as a role model to follow his steps] is earned through patience and certainty; He said,

وَجَعَلْنَا مِنْهُمْ أَئِمَّةً يَهْدُونَ
بِأَمْرِنَا لَمَّا صَبَرُوا وَكَانُوا بِآيَاتِنَا يُوقِنُونَ ﴿٢٤﴾

"And We made from among them leaders guiding by

---

[1] *Ṣabr*: patience and steadfastness, the restraint of ones self to that which is dictated by the divine law. It is of three levels, steadfastness in the obedience of Allāh, steadfastness in avoiding the prohibited matters and patience at the onset of calamity. *Ikhlāṣ* can never be complete without *ṣidq* and *ṣidq* can never be complete without *ikhlāṣ* and the two can never be complete without *ṣabr*. The person is patient through Allāh, i.e. seeking His aid Alone; for Allāh, i.e. arising out of love for Him and the desire to draw close to Him; and with Allāh, i.e. doing only that which He wills.

[2] *Yaqīn*: certainty. It is to faith (*Īmān*) what the soul is to the body, it is the soul to the actions of the heart which in turn formulate the souls to the actions of the limbs and through it one attains the rank of Ṣiddīq. From *yaqīn* does *tawakkul* (absolute reliance in Allāh) sprout and through *yaqīn* is all doubt, suspicion and worry dispelled and the heart filled with love, hope and fear of Allāh. *Yaqīn* is of three levels, that which arises from knowledge (*ʿilm al-yaqīn*), seeing (*ʿain al-yaqīn*) and actual experience (*Ḥaqq al-yaqīn*).

Our command when they were patient and [when] they were certain of Our signs."

[*al-Sajdah* (32): 25]

It is therefore with patience and certainty that a person can reach the status of *al-imāmah* in religion. [Scholars offered different interpretations of what patience refers to in the *ayah*]; some said it is to be patient with respect to this worldly life [i.e. abstain with perseverance from unlawful and sinful worldly pleasures], and some said it is to be patient with the hardships that befall, and some said it is to avoid the unlawful with perseverance. The correct interpretation, however, is that it is to have perseverance over all that; to perform the obligations that Allāh ordained on us with perseverance, to avoid all that which Allāh forbade with perseverance, and to have perseverance over all that which Allāh decreed and predestined for us.

Allāh, Most High, combined patience with certainty in the said *ayah* because the source of happiness of Allāh's slaves emanates from them and without them Allāh's slaves become detached from it. This is because the heart is [often] exposed to the knocks of the sinful desires that contravene Allāh's orders, and to the knocks of the doubts that contravene the divine revealed texts, *however, with perseverance such desires* (al-shawahāt) *are casted away and with certainty such doubts* (al-Shubahāt) *are pushed out* - for [sinful] desire (*al-Shahwa*) and doubt (*al-shubah*) oppose all the aspects of religion. Only those who pushed away their desires with perseverance (*al-ṣabr*) and barred their doubts with certainty (*al-yaqīn*) will be saved from Allāh's punishment i.e. Allāh, Most High, said in the *ayah*,

كَالَّذِينَ مِن قَبْلِكُمْ كَانُوٓاْ أَشَدَّ مِنكُمْ قُوَّةً وَأَكْثَرَ
أَمْوَٰلًا وَأَوْلَٰدًا فَٱسْتَمْتَعُواْ بِخَلَٰقِهِمْ فَٱسْتَمْتَعْتُم بِخَلَٰقِكُمْ

كَمَا ٱسْتَمْتَعَ ٱلَّذِينَ مِن قَبْلِكُم بِخَلَٰقِهِمْ وَخُضْتُمْ
كَٱلَّذِى خَاضُوٓا۟

"[You disbelievers are] like those before you; they were stronger than you in power and more abundant in wealth and children. They enjoyed their portion [of worldly enjoyment], and you have enjoyed your portion as those before you enjoyed their portion, and you have engaged like that in which they engaged. [It is] those whose deeds have become worthless in this world and in the Hereafter and it is they who are the losers."

[*al-Tawbah* (9): 69]

The part *"enjoyed their portion of worldly enjoyment"* refers to their enjoyment of their share of [sinful] desires while the part *"engaged [in vanities] like that in which they engaged"* refers to engaging in false and unlawful matters regarding the religion of Allāh - refering to vain and false topics of the people of doubts. The end of the *ayah*,

أُو۟لَٰٓئِكَ حَبِطَتْ أَعْمَٰلُهُمْ
فِى ٱلدُّنْيَا وَٱلْءَاخِرَةِ ۖ وَأُو۟لَٰٓئِكَ هُمُ ٱلْخَٰسِرُونَ ﴿٦٩﴾

[It is] those whose deeds have become worthless in this world and in the Hereafter, and it is they who are the losers."

[*al-Tawbah* (9): 69]

Allāh mentioned that the result of such a state, namely becoming losers and their deeds becoming worthless, depends on their following of desires, which is enjoying their portion of worldly pleasures, and on following the doubts, which is engaging in false and in vain topics.

# Chapter Two

# Guiding people and calling them to Allah and His Messenger (Peace and Blessings Be Upon Him)

Aside from the two previously mentioned requirements [i.e. patience and certainty], the *ayah* brings to attention two other principles, the first of which is: calling people to Allāh and guiding them, and the second one is: guiding people to Allāh according to what He ordained and ordered through His Messenger (ﷺ), and not according to their intellect, opinions, policies, preferences, and blind following of their forefathers without having an evidence from Allāh. This is because Allāh said, in its meaning,

وَجَعَلْنَا مِنْهُمْ أَئِمَّةً يَهْدُونَ
بِأَمْرِنَا لَمَّا صَبَرُوا وَكَانُوا بِآيَاتِنَا يُوقِنُونَ ﴿٢٤﴾

> "And We made from among them leaders guiding by Our command when they were patient and [when] they were certain of Our signs."
>
> [*al-Sajdah* (32): 24]

To recap, the *ayah* includes four principles.

1) Patience (*al-ṣabr*), which means to withhold oneself from

what Allāh made unlawful, to dedicate oneself in fulfilling what Allāh made obligatory and ordained, and to avert oneself from complaining or being angry at Allāh's decrees.

2) Certainty (*al-yaqīn*), which means to have a profound established faith (*īmān*)[1] - that is free of questions, hesitation and doubts, in five tenets that Allāh stated in the *ayah*,

۞ لَّيْسَ ٱلْبِرَّ أَن تُوَلُّوا۟ وُجُوهَكُمْ قِبَلَ ٱلْمَشْرِقِ وَٱلْمَغْرِبِ وَلَٰكِنَّ
ٱلْبِرَّ مَنْ ءَامَنَ بِٱللَّهِ وَٱلْيَوْمِ ٱلْءَاخِرِ وَٱلْمَلَٰٓئِكَةِ وَٱلْكِتَٰبِ
وَٱلنَّبِيِّۦنَ

"Righteousness is not that you turn your faces toward the east or the west, but [true] righteousness is [in] one who believes in Allāh, the Last Day, the Angels, the Book, and the Prophets."

[*al-Baqarah* (2): 177]

وَمَن يَكْفُرْ
بِٱللَّهِ وَمَلَٰٓئِكَتِهِۦ وَكُتُبِهِۦ وَرُسُلِهِۦ وَٱلْيَوْمِ ٱلْءَاخِرِ فَقَدْ ضَلَّ
ضَلَٰلًۢا بَعِيدًا ﴿١٣٦﴾

"And whoever disbelieves in Allāh, His angels, His books, His messengers, and the Last Day has certainly gone far astray."

---

[1] *Īmān*: The firm belief, complete acknowledgement and acceptance of all that Allāh and His Messenger have commanded to have faith in, submitting to it both inwardly and outwardly. It is the acceptance and belief of the heart that includes the actions of the heart and body, therefore it encompasses the establishment of the whole religion. This is why the Imāms and Salaf used to say, 'Faith is the statement of the heart and tongue, action of the heart, tongue and limbs.' Hence it comprises statement, action and belief, it increases through obedience and decreases through disobedience. It includes the beliefs of faith, its morals and manners and the actions demanded by it.

And it is also stated in the *ayah*,

ءَامَنَ ٱلرَّسُولُ بِمَآ أُنزِلَ
إِلَيۡهِ مِن رَّبِّهِۦ وَٱلۡمُؤۡمِنُونَۚ كُلٌّ ءَامَنَ بِٱللَّهِ وَمَلَٰٓئِكَتِهِۦ وَكُتُبِهِۦ
وَرُسُلِهِۦ

"The Messenger has believed in what was revealed to him from his Lord, and [so have] the believers. All of them have believed in Allāh and His angels and His books and His messengers."

[*al-Baqarah* (2): 285]

Wherein believing in the Final Day is part of believing in the divine Books and Messengers.

Umar ibn al-Khaṭṭāb (*raḍiyAllāhu ʿanhu*) narrated that the Prophet (ﷺ) said: "Faith (*al-īmān*) is to believe in Allāh, His Angels, His Books, His Messengers and the Last Day."[2]

Therefore whoever does not believe in all of the five tenets is not a believer. As for certainty, it is the state when belief in all these five tenets is so profound to the point that the heart can realise the five tenets and observe them just like how the eyes can see the reflection of the sun and the moon [on water]. This is why some of the righteous predecessors said, "Certainty is from Faith."

3) Guiding people and calling them to Allāh and His Messenger: Al-Ḥasan al-Baṣrī used to comment after reciting the *ayah*,

---

[2] Bukhārī (1/22) and Muslim (1/36)

وَمَنْ أَحْسَنُ قَوْلًا مِّمَّن دَعَا إِلَى اللَّهِ وَعَمِلَ صَالِحًا وَقَالَ
إِنَّنِي مِنَ الْمُسْلِمِينَ ﴿٣٣﴾

> "And who is better in speech than one who invites to Allāh and does righteousness and says, 'Indeed, I am of the Muslims.'"
>
> [*al-Fuṣṣilāt* (41): 33],

> "This is the one whom Allāh loves, this is the *walī* of Allāh; he submitted to Him, obeyed Him, done righteous deeds, and called people to Him."

These type of a people are the best of people whose ranks will be the highest on the Day of Judgment. They are the ones whom Allāh exempted from the being losers when He said,

وَالْعَصْرِ ﴿١﴾ إِنَّ الْإِنسَانَ لَفِي خُسْرٍ ﴿٢﴾ إِلَّا الَّذِينَ آمَنُوا
وَعَمِلُوا الصَّالِحَاتِ وَتَوَاصَوْا بِالْحَقِّ وَتَوَاصَوْا بِالصَّبْرِ ﴿٣﴾

> "By time, Indeed, mankind is in loss, Except for those who have believed and done righteous deeds and advised each other to truth and advised each other to patience."
>
> [*al-ʿAṣr* (103): 1-3]

In this *Sūrah*, Allāh swore that mankind is in loss except those who perfect themselves with belief and righteous deeds, and perfected others by advising them about belief and good deeds.

Imām al-Shāfiʿī said, "If people contemplated on *Sūrah al-ʿAṣr*, it would have sufficed them."

A person cannot be a true follower of Allāh's Messenger

unless he calls to Allāh with a *baṣīrah* for the *ayah*,

قُلْ هَٰذِهِۦ سَبِيلِىٓ أَدْعُوٓا۟ إِلَى ٱللَّهِ ۚ عَلَىٰ بَصِيرَةٍ أَنَا۠ وَمَنِ ٱتَّبَعَنِى

"Say, 'This is my way; I invite to Allāh with *baṣīrah*, I and those who follow me.'"

[*Yūsuf* (12): 108]

wherein Allāh used the words,

أَدْعُوٓا۟ إِلَى ٱللَّهِ

"I invite to Allāh"

to explain the way upon which Allāh's Messenger (ﷺ) is; hence inviting to Allāh must be his way and the way of his followers and so whoever does not invite to Allāh will not be upon the way of Allāh's Messenger. As for the part *baṣīrah*,

عَلَىٰ بَصِيرَةٍ

"with insight",

it refers to standing firm in the religion, as Ibn al-'Arabī said. It was also said to mean, "a lesson and an example."

The correct view however, after investigation is that a learned lesson is the fruit of having an insight about a matter because if a person has an insight about something, then he will come to realise the moral behind it; thus whoever does not know the moral or the lesson from a matter it is as if he has no insight.

[In Arabic language], the origin of the word *baṣīrah* means elucidation and appearing; Allāh, Most High, described the Qur'ān to be *baṣāir* (i.e. plural of *baṣīrah*)[4], which translates to the evidence, the guidance and the elucidation leading to the truth and the right course. It is for this reason Arabs call the traces of blood leading to the hunted prey a *baṣīrah*. The *ayah* also indicates that whoever does not have this quality (i.e. *baṣīrah*) is not from the followers of the Prophet (ﷺ), and states that his followers are those with *baṣīrah* as noted in the part

أَنَا۠ وَمَنِ ٱتَّبَعَنِي

"I and those who follow me"

because if the intended meaning is supposed to be *"I and others invite to Allāh"*, and the part

مَنِ ٱتَّبَعَنِي

"those who follow me"

is connected to the noun in

أَدْعُوٓا۟

"I invite",

and that the conjunction in place is deemed good to separate between the two lines, then it is evidence that the followers of the Prophet (ﷺ) are those who invite to Allāh and to His Messenger. On the other hand, if it was associated with the pronoun in

سَبِيلِيٓ

"My way",

It would mean, this is my way and the way of those who follow

[3] See *Sūrah al-Jāthiyah*, verse 21

me. Thus, in both cases, the way of the Prophet (ﷺ) and the way of his followers is to invite people to Allāh.

4) The part of the *ayah*,

يَهۡدُونَ بِأَمۡرِنَا

"Guiding by Allāh's Command"

presents the fourth principle and it proves *that they follow what Allāh revealed to His Messenger, and that their guidance cannot be unless they only comply with the guidance of Allāh's commands*, and not with any opinion or views, because they guide by His command only. This is to show that the Imāms of religion, whom people follow as their leads and examples, are those who have the qualities of patience, certainty and invite to Allāh according to the Sunnah and Allāh's revelation and not according to their opinions and innovations. Truly, those are the successors of the Prophet in this nation; the favoured group that Allāh loves and draws close to Him; hence being their enemy means showing enmity to Allāh, Most High, so Allāh will declare war against His enemies accordingly.

Imām Aḥmad said in the introduction of his book *"refuting the Jahmiyyah"*[4], the following: "All praise is due to Allāh Who facilitated for every era some people of knowledge to guide the astray to the right path and show patience over their harm, to help the blind [hearts] to see with the light of Allāh, and to revive the dead

[4] A group named after Jahm ibn Ṣafwān, who denied the Names and Attributes of Allāh, the Most High. His beliefs were contray to that of *Ahul-Sunnah-wal Jammah*.

[hearts] with the book of Allāh for many [hearts] that Iblīs has assassinated but they managed to revive; and many are those who were astray and lost but they succeeded to guidance. Truly, their effect on people is good and praiseworthy whereas the effect of people on them is vile. They negate what extremists interpolate from the Qur'ān, rebut the claims of falsifiers, and refute the interpretations of the ignorant ones who raised the flags of innovations and unleashed unjustified argumentation, causing them [i.e. ignorant and falsifiers] to depart from the book of Allāh and agree to talk about Allāh and His book without knowledge, and indulge in discussions about the *mutashibhāt* (i.e. verses that are unspecific whose interpretation and meanings are vague), and further they deceive laypeople with their arguments. We seek refuge with Allāh from the nuisances and deviation of people who are astray and misguide others."

# Chapter Three

# Steps in Attaining Happiness

Amongst the matters that people ought to be concerned with and *acquire the knowledge* and cognition thereof, while ensuring to have the will and intent to achieve all that, is to know that human beings, let alone all other living creatures, are after provisions of pleasure, comfort and good life. Through which they can avert the opposite of what they hope to achieve. Evidently, this is a purpose that all creatures are required to achieve and have a sound objective to pursue. This purpose requires the following six steps mentioned below:

1. To know that which is suitable and bring forth benefits through which a person can attain pleasure and comfort and lead a good life.
2. To know the path leading to it.
3. Embarking upon the path.
4. To know that which causes harm and consequently disturbs one's life.
5. To know the path leading to it.
6. To avoid such a path.

Only by following these steps can happiness, pleasure and righteousness can be perfected and assured, otherwise; if either or all the six steps are not followed, one's life will be disturbed and negatively affected. While each sensible person endeavors to act by these six directives, most of them fail to achieve the desired benefit (and result) they pursue - either due to their failure to have the right perspective and knowledge about it, or due to their failure to know the path leading to it. The reason by which people fall in these two errors is ignorance, and acquiring the knowledge will solve the issue.

In some cases, a person may have the knowledge of things that are suitable and bring about benefits, and also knows the path leading to it, yet it happens that he has whims and desires hindering his efforts to achieve the good benefit he is after, and it prevents him from embarking its path because every time he wants to seek it, his whims and desires stand in his own way. However, to overcome his whims and desires freeing him to proceed to achieving the benefit, he must either have an *overwhelming love* or that he *endures an annoyance.*

In the case of the former, he must love Allāh, His Messenger, the Hereafter, Paradise and its bounties more than his own whims and desires, while knowing that he cannot combine both. Therefore he decides to favour the things that he loves the most over the things he loves the least. In the case of the latter, he could have the knowledge of the consequences of favouring his whims and desires; hence he's aware that going along with his whims and desires will cause him lasting fear and pain that last longer and are more severe than the suffering he will endure due to abandoning his whims and desires. If these two types of love take over his heart they will make him realise what should be favored because human intellect directs us to favour the most beloved over the least beloved, and to endure the least disliked in getting rid of the most disliked. By knowing this principle, you will understand the mindset of people and help yourself in distinguishing the sensible from the insensible, and recognise the different levels of people's sensibility. Truly, a person who favours a current pleasure, whose effect will disturb his life and Hereafter, must be a person with no sense of sensibility. For how can a person favour such pleasures that are as temporary as a dream and as short as a good moment a person spends with a character visiting him in a dream, over an everlasting pleasure that is among the ultimate pleasures!

How could a person sell all that for such mortal lowly pleasures that come with pain and are also achieved with pain and whose result is nothing but pain! If the sensible thinks of pain vis-a-vis pleasure and harm vis-a-vis benefit when thinking of such desires, he would have been ashamed of himself and his sensibility; thus he will never pursue such desires or waste his time busying himself with it, let alone favour them over "what no eye ever saw and no ear ever heard of and nor even thought of by any person."[1]

Indeed, Allāh, Most High, has purchased from the believers their lives in exchange for that which they will have in Paradise, and established this contract through His Messenger, the best of mankind whom He loves and favours the most over all other creation. Therefore, how could a sensible person neglect, waste or undermine a merchandise that the Lord of the heavens and the earth has purchased; whose price is to enjoy seeing His Noble Face and hear His Words in Paradise; notwithstanding the great honour of such a contract for being established through His Messenger! How could a person waste this great blessing and settle for a mortal life! Truly, this is the greatest of all loss, which will become evident to such a person on the Day of Judgment when the scales of the pious are heavy and the scales of the losers are light.

---

[1] Bukhārī (4/103) and Muslim (4/2174).

# Chapter Four

# True Happiness and Delight

If you come to know what I have just explained, you will then know that the ultimate pleasure, perfect delight and rejoice, grace and good life are found only in *knowing Allāh, worshipping Him alone, feeling comfort and affability while being with Him, longing* (shawq) *to meet Him, and devoting the heart* (al-qalb) *and endeavors for Him.*

In contrast, the most pettish life is of those whose hearts are distracted [with worldly pleasures] and whose attention [is not devoted to Allāh]; hence they find no abode where they can settle and no beloved to find refuge with. Indeed, a good and beneficial life, with peace of mind are attained through the tranquility and comfort found while being in the company of the first love [i.e. Allāh], no matter how much the heart swings between all the worldly pleasures one loves and desires, it will never enjoy any of them until one feels comfort and safety and delight with his Lord; the only Supporter and Protector whose authority surpasses [all] the creation and without whom no support or protection can be achieved.

You must ensure that you only care about one thing - namely working for the pleasure of Allāh alone, for indeed it is the ultimate happiness that a servant of Allāh can ever dream of having. This is because a person whose heart is in such a state will not only bask in heaven while still being on earth, but will thereafter dwell in Allāh's Paradise in the Hereafter. It was said by one of those whose heart is overwhelmed with the love of Allāh, Most High.

"Sometimes, my heart experiences an overwhelming state [due to being in the company of Allāh] that makes me exclaim, if the dwellers of Paradise experience such a state of happiness and comfort, I am confident that they lavish in a delight beyond imagination."

Another person said, "Sometimes, the heart experiences a state of joy because of which it leaps with great merriment."

And another person said, "How pity and poor are those whose concern revolves around this worldly life! They depart it [the worldly life] without tasting the best of its pleasures." He was asked, and what is that? He replied, "Knowing Allāh, loving Him and feeling affability while being close to Him, and longing to meet Him."

Truly, there is no grace equivalent to the grace that the dwellers of Paradise lavish themselves with except this kind of grace. This is why Allāh's Messenger (ﷺ) said, "Women and fragrance have been made dear to my affections, and my pleasure, peace and contentment are made in the *ṣalāh*."[1]

---

[1] Aḥmad and others
It was declared ḥasan by al-Albānī

In this report, the Prophet (ﷺ) informs us that two things from this worldly life were made dear to his affection, then he followed it with a statement to say that his pleasure, contentment and peace were made for him in the *ṣalāh*. Evidently, the feelings of pleasure contentment and peace are of a higher rank than the feelings of love because not all that a person loves results with pleasure, peace and contentment for such feelings are only attained with the most beloved one, who is beloved for his essence.

This ultimate state of love cannot be for anyone but Allāh alone, the One and only worthy of worship while anything or anyone else is beloved as a result of loving Him; hence persons or things are beloved for His sake and we do not love anyone or anything alongside Him. This is because to love for His sake is a matter of *tawḥīd* [2] whereas to love anything or anyone with Him is [a form of] *shirk*. Because, a *mushrik* (i.e. one who associates partners with Allāh) takes other than Allāh as equals [to Him] and so he loves them as he [is supposed to] love Allāh; whereas a *muwāhid* [i.e. one who worships Allāh alone] loves those whom Allāh loves and hates those whom Allāh hates; all his actions are for His sake and all that which he refrains from are also for His sake.

## [i. Religion revolves around four rules]

Religion revolves around these four rules, namely love (*al-ḥabb*) and hate (*al-bughd*), which necessitates the following actions (*al-fi'l*): refraining and abandoning (*al-tarq*), giving away [that which one

[2] *Tawḥīd*: unification, monotheism, the belief in the absolute Oneness of Allāh. It is to believe that Allāh Alone is the creator, nourisher, and sustainer of the worlds; it is to believe that Allāh Alone deserves to be worshipped; and it is to believe that He has Unique and Perfect Names and Attributes that far transcend anything that one can imagine.

owns] and withholding [i.e. refrain from disbursing]. That being said, whoever ensures all that is sincerely for Allāh's sake, his faith will be perfect and whoever fails to ensure either or all of the said aspects are for Allāh's sake, his faith becomes effected accordingly.

The intended meaning is that, whatever brings forth pleasure, contentment and peace is superior to what we merely like or love - i.e. performing the *ṣalāh* brings forth pleasure, contentment and peace to the ardent devotees who love Allāh in this world due to the fact that *ṣalāh* includes communicating with the only One to whom the hearts are content and exuberated, souls are settled and minds are at peace; it allows them to bask in the grace of remembering Him. It dips their hearts in the ocean of humility and submission to His Majesty, and it draws them near to Him, particularly during the state of prostration which is the closest point a believing slave can be to Allāh. This meaning manifests in the words of the Prophet (ﷺ) when he said: "O Bilāl! Summon [people] to the *ṣalāh* so we can be at comfort and ease by praying."[3]

This statement informs us that the comfort of the Prophet (ﷺ) is found in the *ṣalāh* wherein he finds peace, contentment and pleasure too, as he also stated. Compare this state with those who say, let us pray so we relieve ourselves from the burden of *ṣalāh*!

Only a true devotee finds peace, contentment and pleasure in the *ṣalāh* while the heedless and neglectful is deprived of all that! In fact, such a person finds the *ṣalāh* a difficulty and a burden that makes him disturbed and troubled when praying, and makes him feel as if he is standing on embers. This is why such a person prefers a *ṣalāh* that is very short and quick as he finds no peace,

[3] Aḥmad (6/501) and Abū Dāwūd (#4985)
It was declared saḥīḥ by al-Albānī

pleasure and contentment in it. Indeed, if a person finds peace, contentment and pleasure in a matter, one will find it too difficult to depart from it. While on the other hand, a person whose heart is empty from the love of Allāh and the Hereafter - is inflicted with the love of this worldly life and its pleasures, finds *ṣalāh* to be the most difficult thing to do and despises it the most when it is long, although he is healthy, has sufficient free time and is not busy with anything else.

It is ought to be known too that the *ṣalāh* that brings forth peace, pleasure and contentment to the heart and mind is the type of *ṣalāh* that consists of six elements:

# Chapter Five

# First Element:

# Sincerity (al-ikklas)

The reason for which a servant [of Allāh] prays and feels encouraged to pray should be his intention to draw closer to Allāh; his love for Him; his wish to seek His pleasure and closeness; his compliance with His Command to pray; hence there is nothing from this worldly life that ever encourages him to pray.

Rather, he prays only to seek the pleasure of his Lord the Most High whom he loves and fears, and whose reward and forgiveness he seeks.

[1] *Ikhlāṣ*: sincerity, to strip oneself of worshiping any besides Allāh such that everything one does is performed only to draw closer to Him and for His pleasure. It is to purify ones actions from any but the Creator having a share in them, from any defect or self-desire. The one who has true *ikhlāṣ* (*mukhliṣ*) will be free of *riyā'*.

# Chapter Six

# Second Element:

# Truthfulness (al-sidq)

A person should empty his heart (*qalb*) from everything of this worldly life so it becomes dedicated to Allāh alone while praying, so one can endeavour to be attentive, performs it in the best manner outwardly and inwardly. This is because the *ṣalāh* has two aspects, an apparent aspect (*ẓāhir*) and a hidden aspect (*bāṭin*); the former (*ẓāhir*) is the visible actions (*al-afāʿl al-mushahada*) and audiable statements (*al-aqwāl al-masmūʿah*) while the latter (*bāṭin*) is the vigilance (*al-murāqaba*) of Allāh and attentiveness (*al-khushūʿ*) while keeping the heart fully dedicated to Him and not distracted by anything or anyone else.

[1] *Ṣidq*: truthfulness, the conformity of the inner to the outer such that the deeds and statements of the person do not belie his beliefs and vice-versa. *Ṣidq* is the foundation of faith and results in peace of mind, lying is the foundation of hypocrisy and results in doubt and suspicion, and this is why the two can never co-exist without being at odds with each other.

al-Junayd was asked as to whether *ṣidq* and *ikhlāṣ* were the same or different and he replied, 'They are different, *ṣidq* is the root and *ikhlāṣ* is the branch. *Ṣidq* is the foundation of everything and *ikhlāṣ* only comes into play once one commences an action. Actions are only acceptable when they combine both.' The one who has true *ṣidq* will be free of self-conceit.

The former is like the station of the body (*manzila al-badan*) of *ṣalāh* while the latter is like station of the soul (*manzila al-rūḥ*); therefore, if the soul is absent then the *ṣalāh* becomes like a body without a soul and the servant must be ashamed of himself for meeting his Master in such a state! This is why the *ṣalāh* is empty of its soul, it is rolled up like how a garment is rolled up then it smashes the face of the one who prayed it then says to him, May Allāh waste you just like how you wasted me!

As for the *ṣalāh* whose hidden and apparent aspects are perfected and completed, it rises up (above) with a light that is as shining bright as the sun light until it is presented to Allāh; He then accepts it. The *ṣalāh* then says to the one who prayed it, May Allāh preserves you just as how you preserved me.

# Chapter Seven

# Third Element:

# Compliance (al-mutaba) and Adherence (al-iqtida)

The third element is to ensure praying according to the way of Prophet (ﷺ) and that his *ṣalāh* conforms to the description of the *ṣalāh* of Allāh's Messenger (ﷺ), and to refrain from the actions, statements or description of *ṣalāh* that people innovated and have not been reported from Allāh's Messenger (ﷺ) or his Companions. A person is to pay no attention to the words of those [people of knowledge] who always seek concessions and only comply with the minimum obligatory aspects, all the while, other [people of knowledge] dispute with them over such understanding and views and so declare what those people deem as optional to be obligatory. It is also possible that they disregard authentic ḥadīths and established acts of Sunnah that oppose what they are upon on the grounds that they are following the *madhhab* of so and so.

Evidently, this is an invalid excuse that Allāh does not accept and also does not relieve a person from responsibility for not practicing the Sunnah after knowing about it. This is because Allāh, Most High, ordered us to obey and follow His Messenger alone and the only case where others are obeyed is when they advocate the orders and ways of Allāh's Messenger (ﷺ). That being said, it should be borne in mind that views of every person can be open for discussion and therefore either accepted or rejected, except the orders and statements of the Prophet (ﷺ) whose words are always final and binding.

Allāh, Most High, swore by Himself that we will not believe until we refer to the Messenger of Allāh to judge on what we dispute over, and then submit and accept his judgment for no person's judgment or submission to any other person will save us from the Punishment of Allāh. And, such response will not be accepted when Allāh asks us on the Day of Judgment,

مَاذَآ أَجَبۡتُمُ ٱلۡمُرۡسَلِينَ ﴿٦٥﴾

"What have you responded to the Messengers?"
[*al-Qaṣaṣ* (28): 65]

for He will certainly ask us about it and demand us to answer Him; Allāh, Most High, said,

فَلَنَسۡـَٔلَنَّ ٱلَّذِينَ أُرۡسِلَ إِلَيۡهِمۡ وَلَنَسۡـَٔلَنَّ
ٱلۡمُرۡسَلِينَ ﴿٦﴾

"Truly, We will ask those whom we sent them the Messengers and We shall also ask the Ones We sent to them"
[*al-A'rāf* (7): 6]

The Prophet (ﷺ) said: "It was revealed to me that you will be tested and asked about me"[1], meaning that we will be asked about

[1] Aḥmad and others
It was declared ḥasan by al-Albānī

him in our graves.

Hence whoever is aware of any act of Sunnah then abandoned it for the sake of someone else's view, he will be questioned about it and then will know the consequences of his actions.

# Chapter Eight

# Fourth Element:

# Station of Excellence (al-ihsan) and Vigilance of Allah (al-muraqaba)

Station of excellence (*al-iḥsān*)[1] renders to mean the state of being vigilant of Allāh (*al-murāqaba*)[2] - that is to say, to worship Him as if you could see Him [watching you]. This state stems from having a perfect belief (*kamāl al-īmān*) in Allāh, His Names and Attributes; to the point that you become as if you can envision Him above His Throne above the heavens; arranging the affairs of the entire creation and issuing His commands that governs the cosmos, all the while, the deeds and souls of His slaves are presented before Him. In this state, a believing servant witnesses all that with his heart, and experiences [the application of] His Attributes and Names; he sees [in his heart and mind] that He is the Sustainer [of all that exists] (*al-Qayyūm*), the Ever-Living

---

[1] *Iḥsān*: beneficence, excellence. To worship Allāh as if one is seeing Him, and knowing that even though one sees Him not, He sees the servant.

[2] *Murāqabah*: self-inspection. The servant having the sure knowledge that Allāh sees him in all circumstances and knows all that he is doing, as such the he does his utmost not to fall into the prohibited matters and to correct his own failings.

(*al-Ḥayy*), the All-Hearing (*al-Samīʿ*), the All-Seeing (*al-Baṣīr*), the All-Powerful and Strong (*al-ʿAzīz*), the All-Wise (*al-Ḥakīm*), and the Commander Who has authority over everything; Who Loves, Hates and Be Pleased; Who angers and does all that He is pleased to do; Who decrees all that He wants while being above His Throne; and nothing or anyone escapes from His Knowledge for He knows that which deceives the eyes and what the breasts conceal.

The state of mindfulness is the foundation from which all the deeds of the heart emanate as it necessitates becoming humble (*al-ḥayāʾ*)[3] and shy (*al-ijlāl*) from Allāh, respectful (*al-taʿẓīm*) to Him, and turning (*al-inābah*)[4] to Him. Furthermore, it calls forth one's love (*al-maḥabba*) of Allāh, fear (*al-khashiya*) of Him, [full] reliance (*al-tawakkul*) on Him, submission (*al-khushūʿ*)[5] to Him and the feeling of humility (*al-dull*). It also ends all the whispers (*al-waswāsa*)

---

[3] *Ḥayāʾ*: modesty, derived from the word *ḥayāt*, or life because it is through modesty that the heart is granted life and it is through the absence of modesty that it dies. It is a state that arises through the servant being aware that Allāh is watching him, having love, fear and awe of Him and thinking little of himself. Al-Junayd said, '*al-Ḥayāʾ* is to recognise the bounties of Allāh and then to recognise ones own shortcomings. Through this a state is engendered which is termed *al-Ḥayāʾ*, the reality of which is that it is a mannerism that prevents one from committing vile actions and from being lax in fulfilling the rights of Allāh.'

[4] *Inābah*: returning. ibn al-Qayyim, *Madārij as-Sālikīn* [1/467] said, '*inābah* comprises four matters: the love of Allāh, submission to Him, turning to Him, and turning away from everything besides Him. A person cannot be said to "penitent" unless he meets all four requirements and the explanation of the Salaf to this word revolves around this. The word also carries the meaning of quickness, returning and precedence; therefore the penitent is rushing to do that which would please his Lord, turning back to Him at every moment and foremost in doing that which He loves.'

[5] *Khushūʿ*: submissiveness, humility.

of devils, casts away the doubts and commits the heart and the mind to become devoted to Allāh alone.

How close a servant is from his Lord depends on his share from the state of *iḥsān*, and because of which, the reward and rank of *ṣalāh* differ from one to another so that the difference between the *ṣalāh* of one person and another can be like the distance between heavens and earth though both perform the *ṣalāh* similarly.

# Chapter Nine

## Fifth Element:

## Acknowledgment of Favor (al-minna) of Allah

It is to acknowledge the infinite blessing for being at the service of Allāh. That your heart and body are deployed to serve Him [alone] - and are only for Allāh, whose Grace and Favour were conferred upon you, to facilitate for you being in such a state [of servitude]. Had it not been for Allāh's Grace and Favour upon you, nothing of that would have occurred, which is something that the companions of the Prophet (ﷺ) acknowledged when they used to repeat a line of poetry, that reads as follows:

'By Allāh, was it not for Allāh,
neither would we have been guided,
nor able to give charity nor perform the prayer'

Allāh, Most High, said:

يَمُنُّونَ عَلَيْكَ أَنْ أَسْلَمُوا ۖ قُل لَّا تَمُنُّوا عَلَيَّ إِسْلَامَكُم ۖ بَلِ اللَّهُ
يَمُنُّ عَلَيْكُمْ أَنْ هَدَاكُمْ لِلْإِيمَانِ إِن كُنتُمْ صَادِقِينَ ﴿١٧﴾

"They consider it a favour to you that they have ac-

> cepted Islām. Say, 'Do not consider your Islām a favour to me. Rather, Allāh has conferred favour upon you that He has guided you to the faith, if you should be truthful.'"
>
> [*al-Ḥujurāt* (49): 17]

It is Allāh who permitted a servant, to become a believer in the first instance. It is Him who facilitated for people to pray, just as Prophet Ibrāhīm (*'alayhis-salām*) said in the *ayah*,

رَبَّنَا وَٱجْعَلْنَا مُسْلِمَيْنِ لَكَ وَمِن ذُرِّيَّتِنَآ أُمَّةً مُّسْلِمَةً لَّكَ

> "Our Lord!, And make us Muslims [in submission] to You and from our descendants a Muslim nation [in submission] to You"
>
> [*al-Baqarah* (2): 128]

and

رَبِّ ٱجْعَلْنِى مُقِيمَ ٱلصَّلَوٰةِ وَمِن ذُرِّيَّتِى

> "My Lord, make me one who establishers the prayer, and [many] from my descendants."
>
> [*Ibrāhīm* (14): 40]

It is therefore a fact that it's the favour (*al-minna*) of Allāh that He conferred upon His slaves to worship and obey Him. Indeed, this is from the greatest of Allāh's graces upon His servant: Allāh, Most High, said,

وَمَا بِكُم مِّن نِّعْمَةٍ فَمِنَ ٱللَّهِ

> "And whatever you have of favour - it is from Allāh"
>
> [*al-Naḥl* (16): 53]

and

وَلَٰكِنَّ ٱللَّهَ حَبَّبَ إِلَيْكُمُ ٱلْإِيمَٰنَ وَزَيَّنَهُۥ فِى قُلُوبِكُمْ وَكَرَّهَ إِلَيْكُمُ
ٱلْكُفْرَ وَٱلْفُسُوقَ وَٱلْعِصْيَانَ ۚ أُو۟لَٰٓئِكَ هُمُ ٱلرَّٰشِدُونَ ﴿٧﴾

"And [remember] when your Lord proclaimed, 'If you are grateful, I will surely increase you [in favour]; but if you deny, indeed, My punishment is severe.'"

[*Fuṣṣilāt* (41): 7]

This element by far is one of the greatest elements and most beneficial for the servant of Allāh; so the more profound the *Tawḥīd* of a person is, the more perfected his share from this element will be. One of the benefits attained from this element is that it prevents the heart from feeling egoistic about the good deeds performed because when a person acknowledges and affirms that Allāh, Most High, is the One who guided the servant to Him and that it is His favour upon the servant that he is a believer, he will consequently not be fascinated by his good deeds or even feel superior to other people because of that; therefore all such debased feelings are instantly removed from his heart and so neither does he talk about them nor feel better than others because of them; and this is the nature of any accepted good deed.

From the other benefits of acknowledging Allāh's favour upon us, is that it makes a person praise the One really entitled and deserving of praise; not praise one self but rather acknowledges the fact that all the praise is due to Allāh alone just as one acknowledges the fact that the grace he basks in and the bounties one is blessed with are from Allāh alone. This benefit manifests the perfection (*tamām*) of one's *tawḥīd* of Allāh.

That being said, a person will never have a firm foothold in the rank (*maqām*) of *tawḥīd,* until after one acknowledges and experiences all what has been said. As soon as one comes to cognize this, one deeply roots his footing on its ground, and as soon as the heart experiences that, one will then reap its fruit that no worldly grace or blessing can ever match, i.e. a person will then lavish in the (*al-maḥabba*) love and intimacy (*al-uns*) of Allāh while basking in the amiability of His company and longing (*al-shawq*) to the moment of meeting Him, and luxuriate in His remembrance and worship. Truly, there is no good in life for a person when the path leading to all that is blocked and when the heart is shunned from all that as a person of this kind is as Allāh described in the *ayah*,

ذَرْهُمْ
يَأْكُلُوا وَيَتَمَتَّعُوا وَيُلْهِهِمُ الْأَمَلُ ۖ فَسَوْفَ يَعْلَمُونَ ﴿٣﴾

> "Let them eat and enjoy themselves and be diverted by [false] hope, for they are going to know."
>
> [*al-Ḥijr* (15): 3]

# Chapter Ten

# Sixth Element:

# Blaming One's Self for Inadequate Efforts

It is to maintain the feeling that your endeavours and efforts to worship Allāh are always inadequate; and that the right of Allāh upon you is greater; therefore your obedience, worship and servitude (*al-ʿubūdiya*) must be greater than what you perform, as the level of your servitude to Allāh must befit His Glory and Power.

If the servants and subjects of kings exhibit high regards (*al-taʿẓīm*), respect (*al-iḥtirām*), reverence (*al-tawqīr*), awe (*al-khashiya*), dread (*al-mahāba*) and sincerity (*al-nuṣḥ*) towards their masters to the extent they dedicate their body-limbs and hearts to serve them, then it befits more that the King of all kings (*Mālik al-Malūk*) and the Lord of the heavens and the earth be treated not only in a similar manner but far more superior.

If a servant (*al-ʿabd*) acknowledges that his state of servitude (*al-ʿubūdiya*) does not fulfil, or is even close to fulfilling the due rights of Allāh upon him. A person will then realise their shortcomings and will thus hasten to seek His forgiveness, apologise for ones deficiencies, inadequate worship and obedience. It is for this reason we are in more need of His forgiveness due to our inadequate worship and obedience than we are in need of asking His reward for the worship and obedience we have performed. There is no pride or credit to be claimed by a person, even if one was able to fulfil all the requirements of his state of servitude (*al-ʿubūdiya*) to Allāh, Most High, because in that case one would only be fulfilling the natural (role) of his status as a servant to his Master, Allāh, Glorified be He, requires. It is obvious that if a servant served his master then he requested from his master a reward for his service, people would have deemed him a fool though in the true terms and sense of reality he is not a truly a slave of another man since mankind is owned and is wholly a servant of Allāh alone from all aspects. That being said, when Allāh rewards His servants for their worship, which they are obligated to perform anyhow - as His servants - then that is due to Allāh's favour and grace that He confers upon them, although they are not entitled to receive any reward.

By understanding this, we can comprehend the meaning of the statement of the Prophet (ﷺ), wherein he said, "No one shall enter Paradise by [the virtue of] his deeds." The companions asked: 'Not even you, O Messenger of Allāh?' He replied: "Not even me, unless Allāh engulfs me with His Mercy and Grace."[1]

[1] Bukhārī #6467 and Muslim #2816-7113 records the ḥadīth of Abū Hurayrah that the Prophet (ﷺ) said, "There is not a single person whose deeds will enter him into Paradise." It was asked, 'Messenger of Allāh, not even you?' He replied, "Not even me, unless Allāh were to envelop me in His mercy."

He also records #2816-7121 on the authority of Jābir that he heard the Messenger of Allāh (ﷺ) saying, "The deeds of any one of you will not enter him into Paradise or save him from the Fire, not even me unless it be through the mercy of Allāh."

The ḥadīth is also recorded on the authority of Abū Saʿīd by Aḥmad #11486; Abū Mūsā, Usāmah ibn Sharīk, Sharīk ibn Ṭāriq, and Asad ibn Kurz by Ṭabarānī, *al-Kabīr* #493-1001-6549-7218-7221. For a detail commentary on this ḥadīth refer to '*The Journey to Allāh*' published by Dār as-Sunnah Publishers, 2007.

Anas ibn Mālik (*raḍiyAllāhu ʿanhu*) related: "On the Day of Judgment, there will be three accounts for each person; one of which includes the records of his good deeds, and one of which is for his bad deeds, and the last of which is for the bounties and graces that Allāh conferred on his servant. The Lord, Glorified be He, will says to His graces and bounties, "take your due rights from the good deeds of My slave." Upon which, the least and smallest grace starts to take its right until no more good deeds are left in his account. Then, it says, O my Lord! I have not yet taken enough good deeds to fulfil my right! At that point, if Allāh wanted to show His Mercy to His slave, He would grant him all His graces and bounties, forgive his sins and double his good deeds."[2]

This report is authentic and verified to be narrated by Anas ibn Mālik (*raḍiyAllāhu ʿanhu*), and it is the clearest evidence on the perfect knowledge of the companions about their Lord and His rights upon them. Needless to add, they also have the most knowledge about the Prophet (ﷺ); his Sunnah and the religion. This report includes a knowledge and cognition that no one can comprehend except those who have insightful hearts and know their Lord, His Attributes, Names and rights upon His slaves. By knowing that, we can understand the ḥadīth, recorded by Imām Aḥmad and Abū Dāwūd and narrated by Zayd Ibn Thābit and Hudhayfah (*raḍiyAllāhu ʿanhum*) as well as others that the Prophet (ﷺ) said, "If Allāh punished the dwellers of the heavens and the earth, He will not have been unjust to them, and if He showed Mercy to them, His Mercy will be better for them than their good deeds."[3]

---

[2] Graded as mawqūf by al-Ḥaythamī in his *'Kashf al-Astār 'al-Zawā'id al-Bazzār'*, 4/120 (#3444)

[3] Abū Dāwūd (5/75) and Aḥmad (6/237)
It was declared ṣaḥīḥ by al-Albānī

# Chapter Eleven

# THe Four Pillars

In order to grasp all the aspects of this state (of being), four things need to be assured, namely a sincere intention (*niyyah ṣaḥīḥah*), an overwhelming capacity (*qūwat al-ʿālīya*), desire (*raghbah*) and fear (*rahbah*).

These four points stand out as the basis of this state, and any deficit in one's *īmān*, conditions, apparent and hidden affairs is due to a shortcoming found in either or all these four pillars. Therefore a sensible person must reflect on these four pillars and ensure in complying with them, and abiding by these four rules, and to make them the guideline for his knowledge, deeds, words and conditions [in life]. It can be said that those who have developed this state could not do so without these four pillars and those who failed, did so only because they have not complied with them.

And, Allāh knows best! Upon Him we rely and depend, and it is His pleasure that we seek, and it is Him Who can help us and all our brethren from the people of Sunnah in complying with these four pillars in terms of knowledge and action. Indeed, He is the One Capable of that and it is Him Who suffices us in everything.

# Appendix One

# The Virtues of Patience

The Messenger of Allāh (ﷺ) said, "Know that great good lies in bearing with patience what you dislike." The narration of 'Umar, the freed-slave of Ghufrah, on the authority of ibn 'Abbās has an additional sentence before this phrase, "If you are able to work deeds for the sake of Allāh, being content and in a state of certainty, do so. If you are unable, know that great good lies in bearing with patience what you dislike."[1]

The meaning of certainty here is to actualise faith in the decree (*Al-Qadr*). This is mentioned explicitly in the narration of his son, 'Alī ibn 'Abdullāh ibn 'Abbās, on the authority of his father which has the additional wording, 'I asked, 'Messenger of Allāh, how can I act with certainty?' He replied, "That you know that what afflicted you could never have missed you and what missed you could never have afflicted you."' However, the isnād is ḍa'īf.

When you have consolidated the topic of certainty, attaining certainty in the heart of the decree and ordainment necessitates the heart being at rest and peace with it. This very meaning is articulated by the Qur'ān:

---

* Taken from 'Legacy of the Prophet' by Ibn Rajab al-Hambalī (p.110-132). Published by Dār as-Sunnah Publishers, Birmingham, U.K, 2009.

[1] Abū Nu'aym, vol. 1, pg. 314

مَآ أَصَابَ مِن مُّصِيبَةٍ فِى ٱلْأَرْضِ وَلَا فِىٓ أَنفُسِكُمْ إِلَّا فِى كِتَٰبٍ مِّن قَبْلِ أَن نَّبْرَأَهَآ ۚ إِنَّ ذَٰلِكَ عَلَى ٱللَّهِ يَسِيرٌ ﴿٢٢﴾ لِّكَيْلَا تَأْسَوْا۟ عَلَىٰ مَا فَاتَكُمْ وَلَا تَفْرَحُوا۟ بِمَآ ءَاتَىٰكُمْ ۗ

"Nothing occurs, either in the earth or in your selves, without its being in a Book before We make it happen. That is so that you will not be grieved about the things that pass you by or exult about the things that come to you."[2]

In exegesis to this verse, Ḍaḥḥāk said, 'He strengthened their resolve: *"so that you will not be grieved about the things that passed you by,"* so grieve not about worldly effects (that have missed you), for We have not decreed them for you. *"Or exult about the things that come to you,"* exult not about the worldly effects that We have granted you for they would never have been held back from you.' This was recorded by ibn Abī al-Dunyā.

Sa'īd ibn Jubayr explained the verse with the words, '*"So that you will not be grieved about the things that passed you by,"* of well-being and affluence, this because you know that it was decreed for you before He even created you.' This was recorded by ibn Abī Ḥātim.

It is in light of this that one of the Salaf said, 'Faith in the decree removes worry and distress.' The Prophet (ﷺ) alluded to this with his words, "Be desirous of all that would benefit you and seek Allāh's aid and do not despair. If you are afflicted with something, do not say, 'If only I had done [this], such and such would have

---

[2] *al-Ḥadīd* (57): 22-23

happened,' rather say, 'Allāh decreed and did what He willed. [Saying], 'If only,' opens [the door to] the actions of Shayṭān."[3]

Alluded to in this ḥadīth is that if one were to, at the onset of affliction, remind one's self of the decree, the whisperings of Shayṭān which lead to worry, distress and sorrow would go away.

Anas said, 'I served the Prophet (ﷺ) for ten years and he never once said to me about something I did, "Why did you do that?" or about something I did not do, "Why didn't you do that?"'[4] He said, 'When one of his family would reprimand me, he would say, "Let him be, if something is decreed, it will happen."' The ḥadīth with this additional wording was recorded by Imām Aḥmad.[5]

Ibn Abī al-Dunyā records with an isnād that is problematic that 'Ā'ishah said, 'The most frequent words of the Prophet (ﷺ) when he came home were, "Whatever matter Allāh has ordained will happen."' He also records, with an isnād that is mursal, that the Prophet (ﷺ) said to ibn Mas'ūd, "Do not worry too much; what has been decreed will happen, and what you are to be provided with will come to you."[6] The ḥadīth of Abū Hurayrah has the Prophet

---

[3] Muslim #2664 on the authority of Abū Hurayrah.

[4] Bukhārī #2768-6038-6911, Muslim #2309

[5] Aḥmad #13418, Bayhaqī, *Shu'ab* #8070 with an isnād meeting the criteria of Bukhārī and Muslim.
cf. Arna'uṭ, *Takhrīj Musnad.*

[6] Bayhaqī, *Shu'ab* #1188, Ibn Abī al-Dunyā, *al-Faraj ba'd al-Shiddah.*
Ibn Ḥajr, *al-Iṣābah*, vol. 1, pg. 104 said that the isnād contained 'Ayyāsh ibn 'Abbās who was ḍa'īf. It was ruled ḍa'īf by Albānī, *al-Ḍa'īfah* #4793. cf. Albānī, *al-Ṣaḥīḥah* vol. 4, pg. 34 who mentions two more weak narrations of this ḥadīth on the authority of 'Umar and Abū Dharr.

(ﷺ) saying, "[Saying], '*Lā ḥawla wa lā quwwata illā bi'llāh*'[7] is a cure for ninety nine ailments, the least of which is worry." This was recorded by Ṭabarānī and Ḥākim.[8]

Actualising this statement necessarily leads to relegating all affairs to Allāh and believing that nothing will happen unless Allāh wills it. Faith in this removes worry and distress. The Prophet (ﷺ) advised a man, saying, "Do not impugn Allāh for something He has ordained for you."[9]

When the servant sees the workings of Allāh's wisdom and mercy through His decree and ordainment and knows that He is not to be impugned for His decree, he will attain contentment at Allāh's ordainment. Allāh, Mighty and Magnificent, says,

مَآ أَصَابَ مِن
مُّصِيبَةٍ إِلَّا بِإِذْنِ ٱللَّهِ ۗ وَمَن يُؤْمِنۢ بِٱللَّهِ يَهْدِ قَلْبَهُۥ

"No misfortune occurs except by Allāh's permission. Whoever has faith in Allāh - He will guide his heart."[10]

---

[7] lit: There is no might nor motion except with Allāh.

[8] Ṭabarānī, *al-Awsaṭ* #5028, Ibn Abī al-Dunyā, *al-Faraj ba'd al-Shiddah*.
Ḥākim #1990 said it was ṣaḥīḥ but Dhahabī pointed out that it had a weak narrator, Bishr. Haythamī, vol. 10, pg. 98 said the isnād contained Bishr ibn Rāfi' who was ḍa'īf. Ibn al-Jawzī, *al-'Ilal*, vol. 2, pg. 348 said that it was not authentic and it was ruled ḍa'īf by Albānī, *Ḍa'īf al-Targhīb* #970-1147

[9] Aḥmad #17814-22717, Bukhārī, *Khalq Af'āl al-'Ibād* #163
Mundhirī, *al-Targhīb* vol. 2, pg. 257, after quoting two chains, said of one of them that the isnād was ḥasan. It was ruled ḥasan li ghayrihī by Albānī, *al-Ṣaḥīḥah* #3334, *Ṣaḥīḥ al-Targhīb* #1307. Arna'ūt said that the ḥadīth was a candidate for being ḥasan.

[10] *al-Taghābun* (64): 11

In exegesis to this verse, 'Alqamah said, 'This refers to a misfortune that befalls a person, but he knows that it is from Allāh so he accepts it and is content.'

In an authentic ḥadīth, the Prophet (ﷺ) said, "There is nothing that Allāh ordains for the believer except that it is good for him. If he encounters times of ease, he is grateful and that is good for him. If he encounters misfortune, he is patient and that is good for him. This only holds true for the believer."[11]

The Qur'ān also proves this,

قُل لَّن يُصِيبَنَآ إِلَّا مَا كَتَبَ
ٱللَّهُ لَنَا هُوَ مَوْلَىٰنَا ۚ وَعَلَى ٱللَّهِ فَلْيَتَوَكَّلِ ٱلْمُؤْمِنُونَ
﴿٥١﴾ قُلْ هَلْ تَرَبَّصُونَ بِنَآ إِلَّآ إِحْدَى ٱلْحُسْنَيَيْنِ ۖ

> "Say: 'Nothing can happen to us except what Allāh has ordained for us. He is our Master and it is in Allāh that the believers should put their trust.' Say: 'What do you await for us except for one of the two best things?...'"[12]

Here, He informs us that nothing could happen to them except what He has decreed. This indicates that, regardless if what they encounter is hard or easy, it is the same to them. He then informs us that He is their Master and whoever is in such a position will not be forsaken by Allāh; indeed He will take charge of effectuating good for him,

---

[11] Muslim #2999 on the authority of Ṣuhayb ibn Sinān

[12] *al-Tawbah* (9): 51-52

فَٱعۡلَمُوٓاْ أَنَّ ٱللَّهَ مَوۡلَىٰكُمۡۚ نِعۡمَ ٱلۡمَوۡلَىٰ وَنِعۡمَ ٱلنَّصِيرُ

"Know that Allāh is your Master, the Best of Masters and the Best of Helpers!"[13]

هَلۡ تَرَبَّصُونَ بِنَآ إِلَّآ إِحۡدَى ٱلۡحُسۡنَيَيۡنِۖ

"What do you await for us except for one of the two best things?..."[14]

i.e. either aid and victory or martyrdom: both are best.[15]

Tirmidhī records on the authority of Anas that the Prophet (ﷺ) said, "When Allāh loves a people, He tries them. Whoever is content will have good-pleasure, and whoever is displeased will have displeasure."[16]

Abū'l-Dardā' said, 'Allāh loves that a [servant] be content with a matter when He ordains it.' Ummu'l-Dardā' said, 'Those who are truly content with the ordainment of Allāh are people who are

---

[13] *al-Anfāl* (8): 40

[14] *al-Tawbah* (9): 52

[15] Ibn Abī Ḥātim and Ṭabarī quote this as the exegesis of ibn 'Abbās and Mujāhid.

[16] Tirmidhī #2396, ibn Mājah #4031.
Tirmidhī said that it was ḥasan gharīb. Mundhirī, *al-Targhīb*, vol. 4, pg. 233 said the isnād was ḥasan or ṣaḥīḥ. Ibn Mufliḥ, *al-Ādāb al-Shar'iyyah*, vol. 2, pg. 181 said that the isnād was jayyid. It was ruled ḥasan by Albānī, *al-Ṣaḥīḥah* #146
Aḥmad #23623-23633-23641 records a similar ḥadīth on the authority of Maḥmūd ibn Labīd with the words, "When Allāh loves a people, He tries them. Whoever is patient, for him is patience and whoever despairs, for him is despair." Arna'ūṭ said that the isnād was jayyid.

content, no matter what is ordained. On the Day of Rising they will have such stations in Paradise as would make the martyrs envious.

Ibn Masʿūd said, 'By Allāh's justice and knowledge did He place relief and joy in certainty and contentment, and worry and distress in doubt and displeasure.' This is also reported as a ḥadīth of the Prophet (ﷺ) but is ḍaʿīf.[18]

'Umar ibn ʿAbdu'l-ʿAzīz would say, 'These invocations have left me with no further needs, only submission to the decree of Allāh, Mighty and Magnificent. He would employ them in supplication frequently, saying, "O Allāh make me content with your ordainment and bless me in your decree to the extent that I would not wish to hasten something I delayed or delay something I hastened."'[19]

Ibn ʿAwn said, 'In both times of ease and difficulty be content with Allāh's decree, it will decrease your distress and serve you better in your pursuit of the Hereafter. Know that the servant will never attain the reality of contentment until his contentment at times of poverty and tribulation is the same as his contentment at times of affluence and ease. How can you go to Allāh to adjudge your affair and then be discontent when you find that His ordainment does not accord to your desires?! It is well possible that, were your desire to come to fruition, you would be destroyed! When His ordainment accords to your desires, you are content, and both cases arise because of your scant knowledge of the unseen. How

[17] Bayhaqī, *Shuʿab* #209, ibn Abī al-Dunyā, *al-Yaqīn* #32 with a ḍaʿīf isnād.

[18] cf. Chapter 8 fn #8

[19] Bayhaqī, *Shuʿab* #227

can you go to Him for judgment when this is your condition! You have not been fair to yourself and neither have you hit the mark with regards to contentment.'

These are fine words. The meaning is that when the servant turns to Allāh, Mighty and Magnificent, to aid him in a decision (*istikhāra*), he should be content with what Allāh chooses for him regardless if it conforms to his desires or not. This is because he, himself, does not know in which course the good lies and Allāh, Glorious is He, is not to be impugned for His ordainment. It is for this reason that some of the Salaf, such as ibn Mas'ūd[20] and others, would order a person who feared that he would not be able to bear a decision which opposed his desires, to add the words, 'in all well-being,' to his *istikhāra* since He could choose trial for him and he not be able to bear it. This has also been recorded from the Prophet (ﷺ) but it is ḍa'īf.[21]

Bakr al-Muzanī narrates that a man would frequently make *istikhāra* and as result was tried and was unable to bear it with patience, instead sinking into despair. So Allāh revealed to one of their Prophets, "Tell My servant that if he lacks due resolve then why does he not ask for My decision [with the words], 'in all well-being'?"

The ḥadīth of Sa'd has the Prophet (ﷺ) saying, "From the good fortune of a servant is His seeking a decision from his Lord, Mighty and Magnificent, and being content with what He ordains. From the misery of a person is his abandoning seeking a decision and his dislike of what He ordains." This was recorded

---

[20] Bayhaqī, *Shu'ab* #205

[21] Ṭabarānī, *al-Kabīr* #10012-10052 on the authority of ibn Mas'ūd and it is ḍa'īf.

by Tirmidhī and others.[22]

There are numerous ways to achieve contentment with the decree:

1. The servant having certainty in Allāh and a firm trust that whatever He decrees for a believer will be good for him. As such he will be like a patient who has submitted to the ministrations of a skilled doctor: such a patient will be content with his ministrations be they painful or not because he has a complete trust that the doctor is doing only that which will be of benefit to him. This is what ibn 'Awn alluded to in his aforementioned words.
2. Looking to the reward that Allāh has promised for contentment. The servant could well be so engrossed in pondering this that he forgets all about the pain he is facing. It is reported that a righteous woman from the Salaf tripped and broke a nail whereupon she laughed saying, 'The delight of His reward has made me forget the bitterness of His pain.'
3. Immersing oneself in love of the One who sends tribulation, constantly being aware of His magnificence, beauty, greatness and perfection which is without limit. The potency of such awareness will cause the servant to drown in it such that he no longer senses pain much in the same way that the women who saw Yūsuf forgot about the pain of cutting their hands.[23] This is a higher station than those previously

---

[22] Aḥmad #1445, Tirmidhī #2151
Tirmidhī said that it was gharīb and that its isnād contained Ḥammād ibn Ḥumayd who was not strong. Arna'ūṭ said that the isnād was ḍa'īf. It was ruled ḍa'īf by Albānī, *al-Ḍa'īfah* #1906

[23] Mentioned in, "When they saw him, they were amazed by him and cut their hands. They said, 'Allāh preserve us! This is no man. What can this be but a noble angel here!'" [*Yūsuf* (12): 31]

mentioned.

Junaid said that he asked Sirrī if the lover senses the pain of tribulation to which he replied, 'No.' In these words, he is alluding to this station. It is in this light that a group of those facing tribulation said, 'Let Him do what He wills with us. Even if He were to cut us up, limb by limb, we would only increase in our love.'

One of them said,

If ardent love tore me apart, limb from limb,
The pain would only increase me in love.
I will remain a prisoner to love,
Until, in the pursuit of your pleasure, I pass away.

Ibrāhīm ibn Adham left his wealth, property, children and servants. While performing *ṭawāf*, he saw his son but did not speak to him. He said,

I migrated from all people for love of You.
I bereaved my dependants that I may see You.
If You tore my limbs apart, in my love
The heart would still long for You.

A group of the lovers such as Fuḍayl and Fatḥ al-Mawṣilī, if they went to sleep without an evening meal and without a lamp being lit, they would cry in joy.

During the winter nights, Fatḥ would gather his family and cover them with his cloak and say, 'You made me go hungry so I have made my family go hungry. You have made me a stranger so I have made my family strangers. This You do with Your beloved and

Your friends, am I one of them? Should I exult in joy?'[24]

They entered upon one of the Salaf who was ill and asked him, 'Is there anything you want?' He replied, 'That whatever He finds most pleasing, I find most pleasing.'[25]

In this light, one of them said,

For Your sake, his punishment is sweet.
For Your sake, his distance is closeness.
You are like my very soul,
Rather, You are more beloved!
Sufficient is it in my love
That I love only what You love.

Abū'l-Turāb composed the following lines:

Be not deceived, the lover has signs.
He has routes to the gifts of the Beloved:
Taking delight at the bitterness of His trial,
Being joyous at all that He does,
His withholding is a gift accepted,
Poverty is honour and generosity, transient.

They entered upon a man whose son had been martyred in Jihād and he wept saying, 'I do not cry at his loss, I only cry when thinking what his state of contentment with Allāh was when the swords struck!'

If Ghaḍā's people wish me dead, so be it

[24] Abū Nu'aym, vol. 8, pg. 192

[25] Dhahabī, *Siyar*, vol. 9, pg. 182 quoting it from Yaḥya ibn Sa'īd al-Qattān.

By Allāh, I have never begrudged the beloved's wish!
I am like a slave to them: I cannot object.

The point here is that the Prophet (ﷺ) enjoined ibn 'Abbās to work deeds while in state of contentment if he was able to. If not, he said, "If you are unable, know that great good lies in bearing with patience what you dislike," this then proves that being content with decrees that are hard to bear is not an obligation but rather a recommendation, a state of excellence. Whoever is unable to be content must instead be patient. Patience is obligatory, it must be present, and it contains great good. Allāh, Most High, has commanded patience and promised a great reward for it:

إِنَّمَا يُوَفَّى ٱلصَّٰبِرُونَ أَجْرَهُم بِغَيْرِ حِسَابٍ ﴿١٠﴾

> "The patient will be paid their wages in full without any reckoning."[26]

وَبَشِّرِ ٱلصَّٰبِرِينَ
﴿١٥٥﴾ ٱلَّذِينَ إِذَآ أَصَٰبَتْهُم مُّصِيبَةٌ قَالُوٓا۟ إِنَّا لِلَّهِ وَإِنَّآ إِلَيْهِ رَٰجِعُونَ
﴿١٥٦﴾ أُو۟لَٰٓئِكَ عَلَيْهِمْ صَلَوَٰتٌ مِّن رَّبِّهِمْ وَرَحْمَةٌ ۖ وَأُو۟لَٰٓئِكَ
هُمُ ٱلْمُهْتَدُونَ ﴿١٥٧﴾

> "Give good news to the patient: those who, when disaster strikes them, say, 'We belong to Allāh and to Him we will return.' Those are the people who will have blessings and mercy from their Lord; they are the ones who are guided."[27]

---

[26] *al-Zumar* (39): 10

[27] *al-Baqarah* (2): 155-157

وَبَشِّرِ ٱلْمُخْبِتِينَ ﴿٣٤﴾ ٱلَّذِينَ إِذَا ذُكِرَ ٱللَّهُ وَجِلَتْ قُلُوبُهُمْ وَٱلصَّٰبِرِينَ عَلَىٰ مَآ أَصَابَهُمْ

> "Give good news to the humble hearted, whose hearts quake at the mention of Allāh, and who are patient in the face of all that happens to them."[28]

al-Ḥasan said, 'The state of contentment is rare, but patience is the recourse of the believer.'[29] Sulaymān al-Khawāṣ said, 'The station of patience is below that of contentment. Contentment is that a person, before the onset of tribulation, is content whether it is present or not. Patience is that a person, after the onset of tribulation, bears it steadfastly.'

The difference between patience and contentment is that patience is to restrain the soul and to prevent it from displeasure while sensing discomfort or pain.[30] Contentment necessitates

---

[28] *al-Ḥajj* (22): 34-35

[29] Abū Nuʿaym, vol. 5, pg. 342 from 'Umar ibn 'Abdu'l-'Azīz

[30] *Ṣabr*: to refrain and withhold. Rāghib said, 'It is to withhold the soul as determined by the Legal Law and the intellect.' Jāḥiẓ said that it is a quality made up of sobriety and courage and Munāwī said that it was the ability to face disturbing and painful circumstances, both physical and mental. It is to withhold the soul from misery and displeasure, the tongue from complaining and the limbs from derangement; it is to remain firm upon the laws of Allāh in all circumstances and to face adversity with the best of conduct.

Ibn Ḥibbān, *Rawḍatu'l-'Uqalā'*, pp. 126-128, said, 'It is obligatory upon the intelligent, in the beginning, to adhere firmly to *ṣabr* at the onset of difficulty and when he becomes firm in this he should then move on to the level of contentment (*riḍā*). If one has not been nourished with *ṣabr* he should adhere firmly to inculcating *ṣabr* in himself (*taṣabbur*) for that is the first stages of *riḍā*.

that the heart readily accept what it is facing and, even if it was to feel some pain at what it is facing, the sense of contentment will lessen it, perhaps even remove it altogether. This is because the heart has felt the soothing breath of certainty and cognisance.[31]

This is why a large group of the Salaf such as 'Umar ibn 'Abdu'l-'Azīz, Fuḍayl, Abū Sulaymān and ibn al-Mubārak would say, 'The person who is content does not desire a state other than the one he is in whereas the patient does.' This state of being is reported from a group of the Companions, amongst whom were 'Umar and ibn Mas'ūd.

'Abdu'l-'Azīz ibn Abū Ruwwād said, 'Amongst the Children of Israel there was a devout worshipper who saw a dream in which he

---

If a man was to have *ṣabr*, truly would he be noble; for *ṣabr* is the fount of all good and the foundation of all obedience... The stages leading to it are concern (*ihtimām*), awakening (*tayakkuẓ*), examination and circumspection (*tathabbut*), and *taṣabbur*; after it comes *riḍā* and that is the peak of the spiritual stations... *ṣabr* is displayed in three matters: *ṣabr* from sin; *ṣabr* upon obedience; and *ṣabr* in the face of adversity and calamity.' cf. Ibn al-Qayyim, *Madārij al-Sālikīn*, vol. 1, pp.162-165

[31] *Riḍā*: the opposite of displeasure and malcontent. Jurjānī said that it referred to the joy of the heart at the occurrence of the decree. Ibn al-Qayyim, *Madārij*, vol. 2, pg. 185 mentioned that it is the tranquillity of the heart in the face of the vicissitudes of the decree and the firm knowledge that it has that Allāh would only that which is good for it.

Bayhaqī, *Shu'ab* #209 records that ibn Mas'ūd (*raḍiyAllāhu 'anhu*) said, '*Riḍā* is that you not please the people at the expense of the displeasure of Allāh; that you not praise anyone for the provision Allāh has granted you; and that you not blame anyone for that which Allāh has not given you. The grant of provision is not dictated by the avarice of a person and neither is it withheld because of the aversion of another. By Allāh's justice and knowledge did He place relief and joy in certainty and contentment, and worry and distress in doubt and displeasure.'

was told that so-and-so would be his wife in Paradise. So he went to her as a guest for three nights to see what she did. She would sleep while he prayed by night and she would eat while he fasted. When he left her, he asked her about the greatest deed she felt she did. She replied, "I do no more than what you have seen except that I have one quality: If I am in trying times, I do not want to be in times of ease. If I am ill, I do not wish to be healthy. If I am hungry, I do not wish to be full. And if I am in the sun, I do not wish to be in the shade." He said, "By Allāh, this is a quality that is beyond the reach of the servants!'"

Patience is to be shown at the onset of calamity as is authentically reported from the Prophet (ﷺ).[32] Contentment is shown after the onset of calamity as the Prophet (ﷺ) said in his supplication, "I ask You for contentment after the decree."[33] This is because a servant could well resolve to be content at the decree before it occurs, but the resolve dissipate when he actually faces it. Whoever is content after the decree has befallen is one who is truly content.[34]

Therefore, in summary, patience is obligatory and must be present. Beyond patience there is displeasure and malcontent and whoever is displeased at the decree of Allāh, his lot will be displeasure. Moreover, the pain he will face and the malice of his enemies will be far greater than his despair, just as one of them said,

---

[32] Bukhārī #1283-1302-7154, Muslim #626 on the authority of Anas

[33] Aḥmad #18325, Nasā'ī #1306-1307 on the authority of ʿAmmār ibn Yāsir It was ruled ṣaḥīḥ by ibn Ḥibbān #1971, Ḥakim #1923 with Dhahabī agreeing, Albānī, *Takhrīj al-Nasā'ī* and Arnaʿūṭ.

[34] cf. Khaṭṭābī, *Sha'n al-Duʿā*, pg. 132

Despair not at any mishap that befalls
Allow not the malice of the enemy free hold
People, through patience will you see your hopes
When you meet the opposing army, stand firm!

The Prophet (ﷺ) said, "Whoever inculcates patience in himself, Allāh will grant him patience. Allāh has not granted anyone a gift better and more expansive than patience."[35]

ʿUmar said, 'The best times of our lives have been those accompanied by patience.'[36] ʿAlī said, 'Patience with respect to faith is like the head with respect to the body: a person who has no patience has no faith.'[37]

al-Ḥasan said, 'Patience is one of the treasures of Paradise. Allāh only confers it to those He ennobles.' Maymūn ibn Mihrān said, 'No Prophet or anyone else has ever attained good except through patience.' Ibrāhīm al-Taymī said, 'Allāh does not gift a servant with patience at harm, patience at tribulation and patience at calamity except that He has conferred on him the best [gift] after faith in Allāh, Mighty and Magnificent.' He derived this from the saying of Allāh, Most High,

---

[35] Bukhārī #1469-6470, Muslim #1053 on the authority of Abū Saʿīd al-Khudrī

[36] Bukhārī as a taʿlīq report. Ibn Ḥajr, *Fatḥ*, vol. 11, pg. 309, said, 'Aḥmad, *Kitāb al-Zuhd* (#117), provided a complete chain to Mujāhid who said that "Umar said...' and it is ṣaḥīḥ.' It is also recorded by ibn al-Mubārak, *al-Zuhd* #630, Wakīʿ, *al-Zuhd* #198

[37] Ibn Abī Shaybah, *al-Īmān* #130, Wakīʿ #199, Bayhaqī, *Shuʿab* #40, Abū Nuʿaym, vol. 1, pp. 75-76
Suyūṭī, *al-Jāmiʿ* #5136 ruled it ḍaʿīf.

۞ لَّيْسَ الْبِرَّ أَن تُوَلُّوا وُجُوهَكُمْ قِبَلَ الْمَشْرِقِ وَالْمَغْرِبِ وَلَٰكِنَّ
الْبِرَّ مَنْ آمَنَ بِاللَّهِ وَالْيَوْمِ الْآخِرِ وَالْمَلَائِكَةِ وَالْكِتَابِ
وَالنَّبِيِّينَ وَآتَى الْمَالَ عَلَىٰ حُبِّهِ ذَوِي الْقُرْبَىٰ وَالْيَتَامَىٰ
وَالْمَسَاكِينَ وَابْنَ السَّبِيلِ وَالسَّائِلِينَ وَفِي الرِّقَابِ وَأَقَامَ
الصَّلَاةَ وَآتَى الزَّكَاةَ وَالْمُوفُونَ بِعَهْدِهِمْ إِذَا عَاهَدُوا
وَالصَّابِرِينَ فِي الْبَأْسَاءِ وَالضَّرَّاءِ وَحِينَ الْبَأْسِ ۗ أُولَٰئِكَ الَّذِينَ
صَدَقُوا ۖ وَأُولَٰئِكَ هُمُ الْمُتَّقُونَ ﴿١٧٧﴾

> "...rather, those with true devoutness are those who have faith in Allāh and the Last Day, the Angels, the Book and the Prophets, and who, despite their love for it, give away their wealth to their relatives and to orphans and the very poor, and to travellers and beggars and to set slaves free, and who establish prayer and pay zakāt; those who honour their contracts when they make them, and are patient in poverty and illness and in battle. Those are the people who are true. They are the people who have *taqwā*."[38]

'Umar ibn 'Abdu'l-'Azīz said, 'Allāh does not grant a blessing to a person only to take it away, leaving patience in its place, except that the replacement was better than what was removed.' Then he recited,

إِنَّمَا يُوَفَّى الصَّابِرُونَ أَجْرَهُم بِغَيْرِ حِسَابٍ ﴿١٠﴾

> "The patient will be paid their wages in full without any reckoning."[39]

---

[38] *al-Baqarah* (2): 177

[39] *al-Zumar* (39): 10

One of the righteous would have a piece of paper which he kept in his pocket. Every hour he would look at it and read it. Written therein were the words,

وَٱصْبِرْ لِحُكْمِ رَبِّكَ فَإِنَّكَ بِأَعْيُنِنَا

"So wait patiently for the judgement of your Lord - you are certainly before Our eyes."[40]

Beautiful patience is a servant's keeping his tribulation to himself and not telling anyone about it. Allāh, Most High says,

فَصَبْرٌ جَمِيلٌ

"But beauty lies in patience."[41]

In exegesis to this, a group of the Salaf said that it referred to patience that was not accompanied by any form of complaint.[42]

Aḥnaf ibn Qays had lost his sight for forty years, yet he told no one. 'Abdu'l-'Azīz ibn Abū Ruwwād became blind in one eye for twenty years, then, one day, his son looked at him carefully and said, 'Father, one of your eyes is blind!' He replied, "Yes my son, for the past twenty years have I been content with Allāh." Imām Aḥmad would never complain of any illness that afflicted him to anyone. It was mentioned to him that Mujāhid would dislike moaning while ill, so he stopped doing it and never did so till the day he died. He would exhort his self saying, 'Be patient or you will regret!'

---

[40] *al-Ṭūr* (52): 48

[41] *Yūsuf* (12): 83

[42] cf. Ṭabarī.
Refer to Appendix 2 for a further discussion on patience by ibn al-Qayyim.

One of the Gnostics visited a sick person who was saying, 'Ah! Ah!' He asked, 'Who from?' One of them said,

The soul is beset with illness
Yet it hides its malady from those who visit
The inner self has not been just if it complains
Of its desires to other than its beloved

Yaḥyā ibn Muʿādh said, 'If you love your Lord and He decreed hunger and nakedness for you, it would be obligatory for you to bear it and withhold it from creation. The lover patiently bears harm from his beloved, so why would you present your complaints to it for something it has not done to you?'

In my view, deeds from any besides You are hateful.
You do acts and they, coming from You, are beautiful.

The Messenger of Allāh (ﷺ) and his Companions would tie rocks to their bellies against the hunger they faced.[43]

Uwais would collect broken pieces of bone from the rubbish heap with dogs crowding around him trying to do the same. One day a dog barked at him and he said, 'Dog, do not harm one who does not harm you, eat what is close to you and I will eat what is close to me. If I enter Paradise, I would be better than you, and if I enter the Fire, you would be better than me.'

Ibrāhīm ibn Adham would collect ears of grain along with the poor. Seeing that they disliked his competing with them in acquiring them, he thought, 'I have abandoned property at Balkh to compete with the poor in collecting grain?' After that he would only ever

---

[43] Bukhārī #6452 on the authority of Abū Hurayrah

gather grain amongst the animals who would pasture in that land.

Imām Aḥmad would collect grain with the poor. Sufyān al-Thawrī was once employed to look after two camels while on the road to Mecca. He cooked food for some people and it tasted so bad that they beat him for it. Fatḥ al-Mawṣilī would build fires for people for a wage.

For Your sake did I leave the land
To the malicious, to the envious.
Master, for how long will I remain in Your good grace
My life rushes by, my need is not fulfilled.

Another said,

Much subjugation and toil have I seen pursuing Your grace.
Much patience have I born for You in the face of illness and frailty.
Abandon me not, I cannot do without You.
If you wish a wage, take my soul.
For Your good pleasure I have born ardent love.
My heart is deeply in love, my tears choke me.
The love of You makes all that I face easy to bear.
A person does not sense blessing if he has not faced hardship.

In their view, the tribulations of this world would be blessings. One of them said, 'The true jurist is one who sees tribulation as a blessing and ease a misfortune.' It is mentioned in a Judaeo-Christian narration, 'If you see someone affluent approaching, say, "A sin whose punishment has been hastened on!" If you see some-one poor approaching, say, "A sign of the righteous, welcome!"'[44]

---

[44] This was said by Shurayḥ al-Qāḍī as per Dhahabī, *Siyar*, vol. 4, pg. 105

One of the Salaf said, 'When I am afflicted with calamity, I praise Allāh four times: I praise Allāh for it not being worse than it is, I praise Allāh for nourishing me with the ability to bear it patiently, I praise Him for granting me the accord to say, "To Allāh we belong and to Him we return,"' and I praise Him for not making the tribulation in my religion.'

Looking to relief through patience is an act of worship since tribulation never remains forever.

Patiently bear every calamity, take heart,
Know that harm never endures forever.
Be patient, just as the nobles were patient:
It is a fleeting event; here today, gone tomorrow.

If the most severely afflicted person were to be dipped but once in the bliss of Paradise and then asked, 'Have you ever seen calamity? Have you ever encountered calamity?' He will reply, 'My Lord, no!'[45]

O soul, patience only for a few days!
Their length? A few flitting dreams!
O soul, pass through this world quickly;
Turn away from it, true life lies ahead!

Another said,

It is only an hour, then it will depart
All of this will go, it will disappear.

---

[45] As mentioned in a ḥadīth recorded by Muslim #2807 on the authority of Anas.

www.ingramcontent.com/pod-product-compliance
Lightning Source LLC
Chambersburg PA
CBHW051900090426
42811CB00003B/406
*9781643544359*